POOL WATER DOESN'T TASTE LIKE A TACO

BOOK 1

UGH! Look at all those tiny words!

POOL WATER DOESN'T TASTE LIKE A TACO
©2023 Michelle Lang
Published by RBL PUBLISHING 2023
Editor: Deborah M. Lang

ISBN Paperback: 978-1-951756-04-8

For additional permissions contact:
RBL@RelaxationBasedLifestyle.com

DEDICATION:

To the thousands of kids I've had the
honor to teach to swim.

For parents:

A MERMAID'S GUIDE:
Empower Your Child in Water and in Life.

A Mermaid's Guide is a modern, holistic swim method focused on giving you pool and parenting tips to help your child love swimming.

Written by Michelle Lang, graduate of Northwestern University, B.S. Communications, WSI (Water Safety Instructor) American Red Cross, and swim instructor to Hollywood's biggest stars since 2006.

Where the Sanity Ends

Hilarious and touching, "Where the Sanity Ends" is a comedic parody of Shel Silverstein's "Where The Sidewalk Ends" for parents. Enjoy humorous prose about important topics like how to smuggle cold brew through airport security, the dearth of lactating men, and the sultry woes of reusable diapers.
Playfully illustrated by U.W. Madison B.F.A., Holli Jacobson.

For kids:

Under the Rug
Join Andy on a quest to discover the TRUTH about what is under the rug. Is it leeches? Cockroaches? Or something far more disgusting altogether?

Under the Rug is sprinkled with challenging vocabulary words, alluring alliteration, and energizing illustrations to help every child fall in love with reading.

Bubble
A bubble soars through the sky to see what it can discover. Along the way, it meets other bubbles that influence how it looks and feels. Will the bubble stay the same, or become a different bubble altogether?

Bubble is a story about how people touch our lives, even after they are gone.

POOL WATER DOESN'T TASTE LIKE A TACO

Art and Words
by
Michelle Lang

I'm Mr. Sharky!

I'm Pufferfish!

RBL Publishing

This is a pool.

Duh.

Always go in a pool WITH a GROWN-UP!

Grown-up!

Grown-up!

TWO grown-ups!

Always swim **with** a grown-up.

ALWAYS swim **WITH** a grown-up. Got it.

If you swim with a grown-up and **if** you take a BIG BREATH...

Then you can go underwater!

Hold your bubbles in your body!

What? We aren't blowing bubbles?

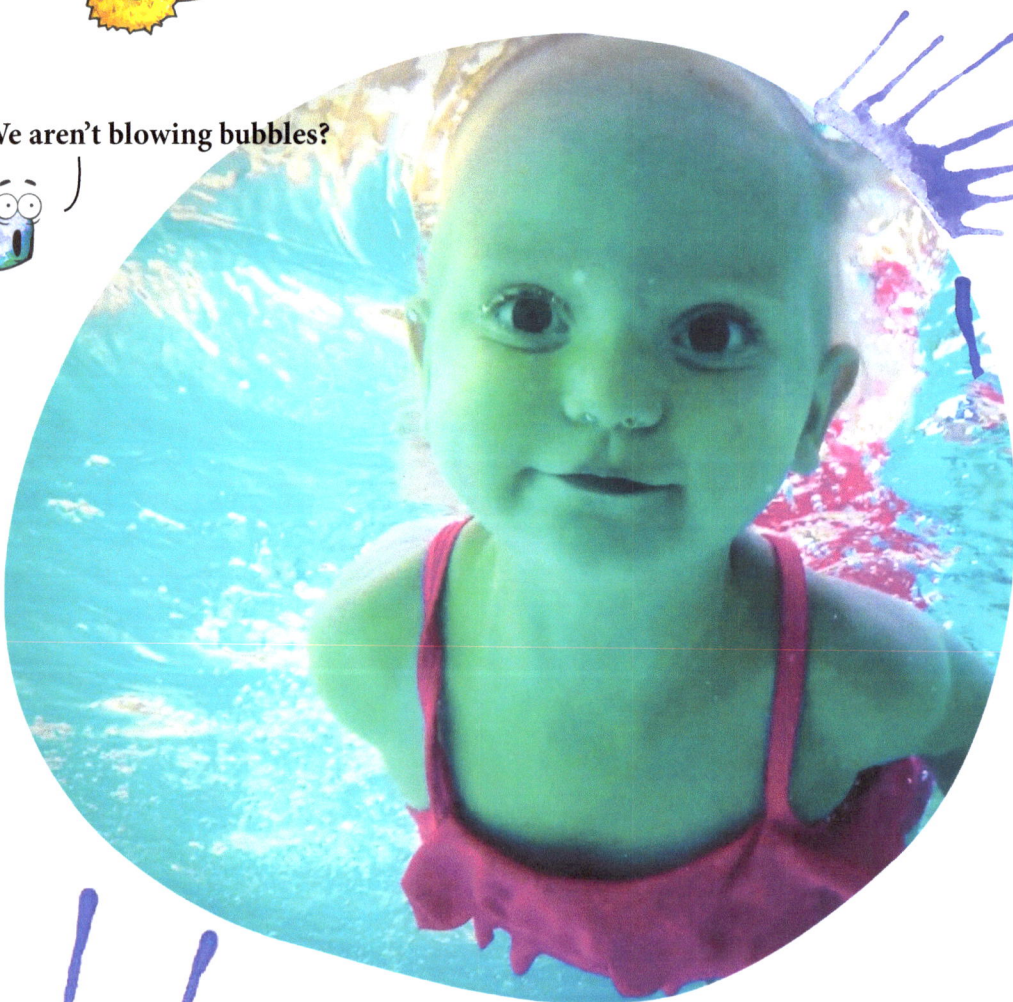

NO bubbles!
Take a big breath and HOLD IT!
Like a pufferfish!

BUT DON'T DRINK THE WATER!

It doesn't taste like a

TACO!

BLAH!!!

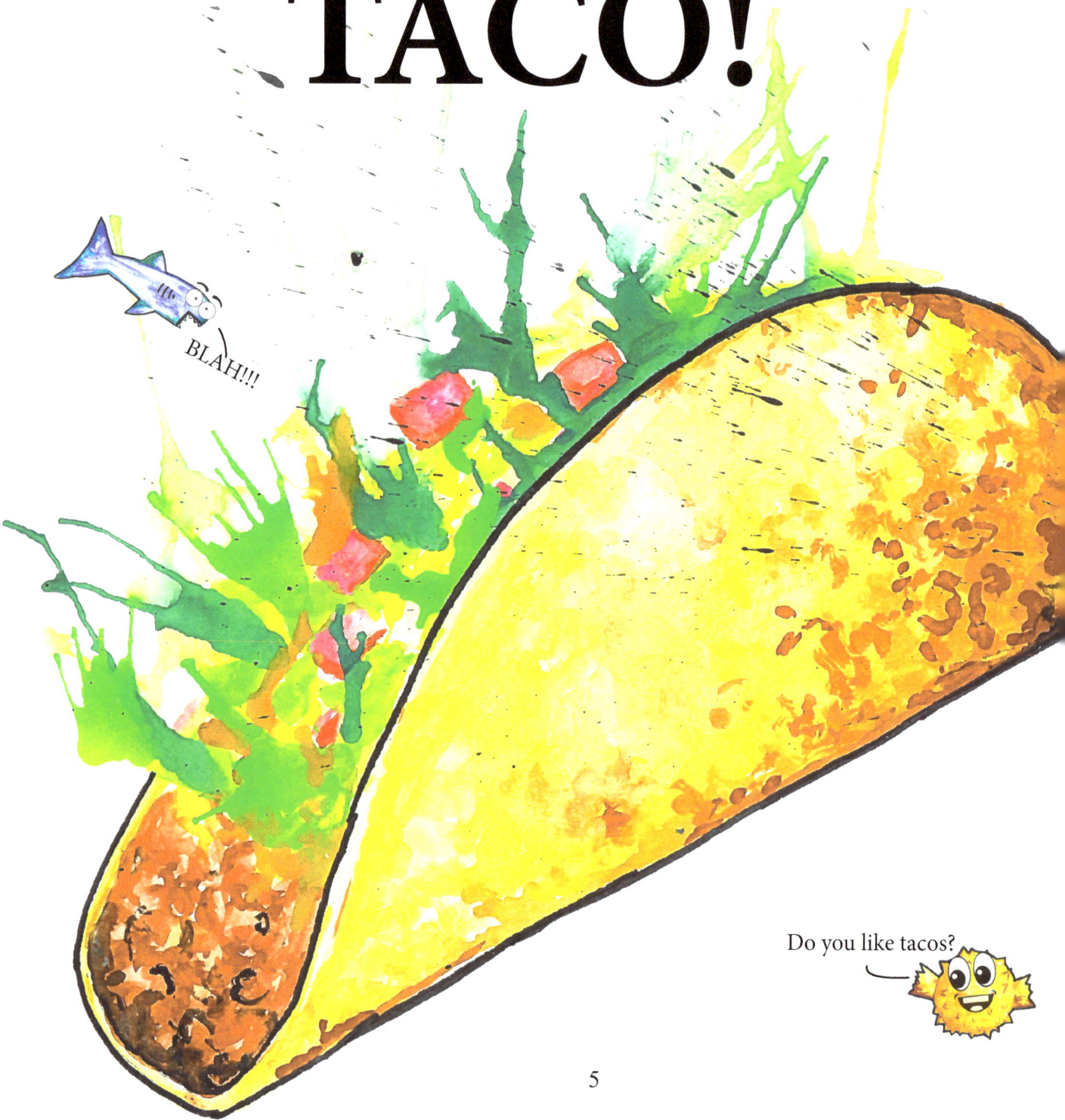

Do you like tacos?

5

If you swim with a grown-up, and **if** you can hold your breath for five seconds...

Then you can float!

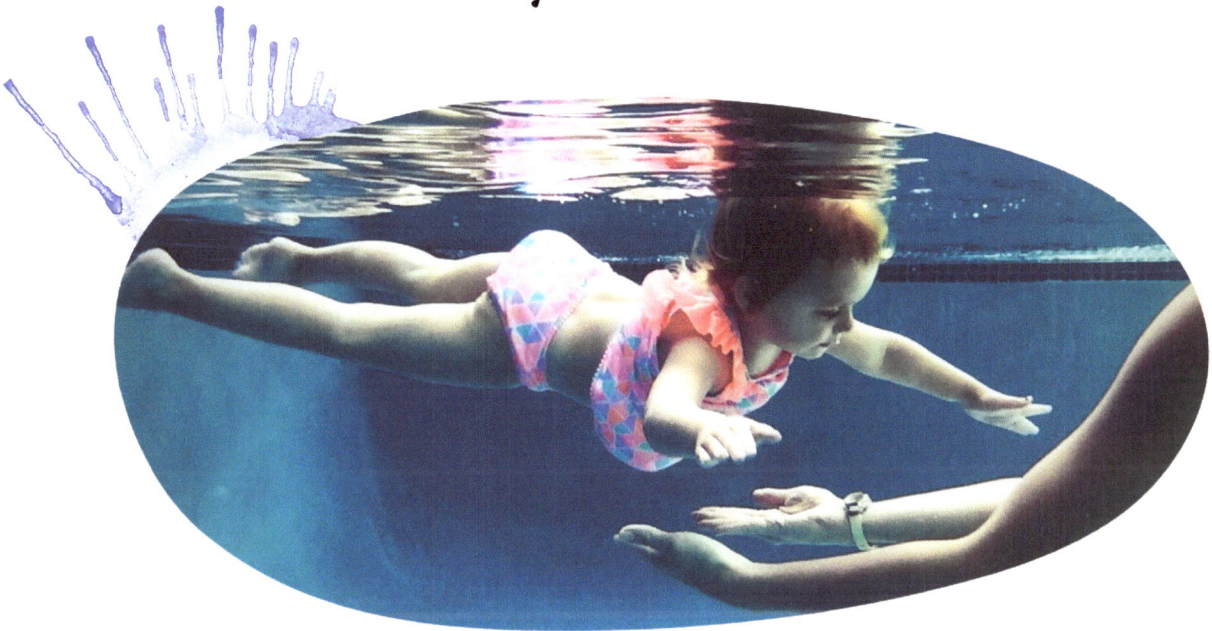

The bubbles in your body help you float!

YES!

Your body is like a BALLOON?

BUT DON'T DRINK THE WATER!

It doesn't taste like a

BANANA

BLAH!!!

Do you like bananas?

8

If you swim with a grown-up
and you put air in your body and float...

Then you can use your kickies to
make you go FAST!

The water holds you up because
you have AIR in your body!

And kickies make you GO FAST!
I LOVE TO GO FAST!!!

BUT DON'T DRINK THE WATER!

It doesn't taste like a...

PICKLE!

BLAH!!!

Do you like pickles?

11

If you swim with a grown-up,
put air in your body,
and use your kickies to make
you go FAST...

Then you can use your arms to REACH
AND PUSH the water out of your way.

REACH!

PUSH!

Isn't this breaststroke arms and flutter kicks?
What kind of crazy stroke is this?

Just trust me, Mr. Sharky!

BUT DON'T DRINK THE WATER!

It doesn't taste like an...

Apple!

BLAH!!!

Do you like apples?

If you swim with a grown-up,
put air in your body,
and use your kickies to
make you go FAST...
Then, if you want to SPIN or TURN, you
LOOK where you want to go and **push**
the water out of your way.

You're the boss of the water.

Push it out of your way!

BUT DON'T DRINK THE WATER!

If you swim with a grown-up,
put air in your body,
use your kickies to make you go FAST,
and **look** where you want to go...

Then, when you need a breath, push the

water down and look **UP** to the sky.

Air is UP!!!

BUT DON'T DRINK THE WATER!

It doesn't taste like a...

STRAWBERRY!

BLAH!!!

Do you like strawberries?

Mr. Sharky's and Pufferfish's 7 rules in the pool.

UGH! RULES! BLAHHHHH!

They are good, I promise!

1. ALWAYS SWIM WITH A GROWN-UP.

2. Take a BIG BREATH before you go under.

3. CLOSE YOUR MOUTH!

Oh geez, there's more?

4. Hold your bubbles in your body and the water will hold you up.

Your body is like a **BALLOON!**

5. *Kickies make you go FAST!*

6. LOOK where you want to go and push the water out of your way.

7. Push the water **DOWN** and look **UP** when you need air.

Fine, those were good.

But most of all...

DON'T DRINK THE WATER!

It doesn't taste like a...

TACO!

BLAH!!!

HEY! What about PIZZA!

I THOUGHT WE WERE
ENDING WITH PIZZA!!!

Calm down, calm down...okay!!!

It doesn't taste like **PIZZA** either.

There, you happy?

Yes. Thank you.

Do you like pizza?

Author's note.

Thank you for reading!
If you would share Pool Water
Doesn't taste Like a TACO
on Social Media, or gift this
book to a child who needs
to learn about the water,
I would be incredibly
grateful.
Xo Michelle Lang

BLAH! So sappy.

Did you know that a review on Amazon.com is SO HELPFUL for independent books?

BLAH! You are asking me to:
1. Go to www.Amazon.com
2. Search for "Pool Water Doesn't Taste like a Taco"
3. Scroll down to "Customer reviews"
4. Click on "Write a customer review"
5. Then WRITE some WORDS?

Yes! The Amazon algorithm will "suggest" the book to more people if you leave a review!

Not happening. I'm sleepy. My 18 shark babies kept me up **all** night with their stuffy gills. I've got dishes to scrub and little shark undies to fold. I'm very busy.

YOUR REVIEW WILL HELP MORE KIDS LEARN ABOUT THE WATER!

Okay, okay. I'll leave a review.

Thank you!

Tag me!

@TheMichelleLang | @AMermaidsGuide
#PoolWaterDoesn'tTasteLikeATaco

Videos on YOUTUBE:
Search: Pocket Noggin

www.ingramcontent.com/pod-product-compliance
Lightning Source LLC
LaVergne TN
LVHW072131070426
835513LV00002B/67